Improve your sight-reading!

A workbook for examinations Grades I-V

BASSOON

JOHN DAVIES AND PAUL HARRIS

FABER **ff** MUSIC

INTRODUCTION

To the Teacher

The ability to sight-read fluently is now more than ever an essential skill for all players, both professional and amateur. Yet the *study* of sight-reading is often badly neglected by young players, and is frequently regarded as no more than an unpleasant side-line in their training. The purpose of this workbook is to incorporate sight-reading into regular practice and lessons, and to help prepare young students for the sight-reading tests in grade examinations. It is intended as a source of motivation, offering a progressive series of enjoyable and stimulating stages in which the student will have the opportunity to show considerable improvement from week to week.

The sight-reading exercises and questions are related to the requirements of the first five graded examinations. An approximate guide to standard is as follows:

Preparatory stage to stage 4	= Grade I
Stages 4 to 6	= Grade II
Stages 6 to 8	= Grade III
Stages 8 to 10	= Grade IV
Stages 10 to 12	= Grade V

Each stage consists of two parts: firstly, two pages of work to be prepared by the student in advance, consisting of preliminary rhythmic and melodic exercises, and then a short piece with related questions; and secondly, an unprepared test. (These tests – three examples for each stage – are to be found at the end of the book.)

The student's work can be assessed using the marking scheme outlined below.

Marking

Each stage carries a maximum of 50 marks:

14 marks maximum for the rhythmic and melodic exercises
1 mark for each of the six questions relating to the prepared piece (total 6)
10 marks for the prepared test.
20 marks for the unprepared test. (You should devise a similar series of questions for the unprepared test, and take the student's answers into account when allocating a final mark.)

Space is given at the end of each stage to maintain a running total so that progress may be clearly observed.

To the Student

The ability to sight-read fluently is a most important part of your training as a player, whether you intend to play professionally, or simply for enjoyment. If you become a good sight-reader you will be able to learn pieces more quickly and to play in ensembles with confidence. Furthermore, in grade examinations, good performance in the sight-reading test will result in useful extra marks.

How to use this workbook

The book is divided into 12 stages and a preliminary stage. Each stage introduces one or more new features, which appear at the top of the left-hand page. Your aim in sight-reading should be to play the notes and rhythms correctly and to observe dynamic levels. You should prepare the exercises in each stage carefully and your teacher will mark your work according to accuracy. There are normally four different types of exercise in each stage:

1 **Rhythmic exercises.** It is very important that you should be able to feel and maintain a steady beat. The purpose of the *rhythmic exercises* will help you develop this ability. Clap or tap the lower line (the beat) while singing the upper line to 'la'. Always clap or tap two bars before you begin the upper line, in order to establish the beat.

2 **Melodic exercises.** Fluent sight-reading depends on recognising melodic shapes at first glance. These shapes are generally related to scales and arpeggios. Thorough knowledge of scales and arpeggios is therefore invaluable in developing fluent sight-reading. Always notice the *key-signature*, and the notes affected by it; and any *accidentals* before you begin.

3 **A prepared piece with questions.** On the next page you will find a short *piece*, which you should also prepare carefully, together with a set of *questions*. The questions are similar to those asked at some grade examinations, and are there to help you think about and understand the piece before you play it. Put your answers in the spaces provided, and your teacher will mark them.

4 **An unprepared piece.** Finally, your teacher will give you an *unprepared* test to be read *at sight*. Make sure you look at the *time-signature*, the *key signature*, *accidentals* and the *dynamic levels*.

Remember to count throughout each piece and to keep going at a steady and even tempo. Always try to look ahead – at least to the next beat.

You will be awarded marks out of a total of 50 for each stage. There is a box provided at the end of each stage so that you can keep a running total of your marks as you progress.

PREPARATORY STAGE

RHYTHMIC EXERCISES

Always note and remember the time- and key-signature.

MELODIC EXERCISES

*The mark boxes are to be filled in by the teacher

*Mark:

This book is copyright. Photocopying is illegal.

PREPARED PIECE

1 How many beats are there in each bar?

2 In which key is the piece written?

3 How many beats is each crotchet (♩) worth?

4 How many beats is each crotchet rest (𝄽) worth?

5 What does *Moderato* mean?

6 What does *f (forte)* indicate?

Total:

Moderato

Mark:

Prepared work total:

Unprepared:

Total:

STAGE 1

C major

RHYTHMIC EXERCISES

1

MELODIC EXERCISES

1

Mark:

PREPARED PIECE

1   What does $\frac{4}{4}$ indicate? How many beats will you count in each bar?

2   How many beats is each crotchet (♩) worth?

3   How many beats is each crotchet rest (𝄽) worth?

4   What are the letter names of the first and last notes of bar 7?

5   What does *f (forte)* indicate?

6   What is the meaning of *Allegretto?*

Total:

Allegretto

Mark:

Prepared work total:

Unprepared:

Total:

STAGE 2

$\begin{array}{c} 3 \\ 4 \end{array}$ 𝅗𝅥 𝅗𝅥.

RHYTHMIC EXERCISES

1

2

3

MELODIC EXERCISES

1

2

3

4

Mark:

PREPARED PIECE

1 What does $\frac{3}{4}$ mean?

2 How many beats is each minim (♩) worth?

3 How many beats is each dotted minim (♩.) worth?

4 What is the letter name of the note in bar 8?

5 What does *mf (mezzo-forte)* indicate?

6 What is the meaning of *Andante?*

Total:

Andante

mf

Mark:

Prepared work total:

Unprepared:

Total:

Running totals:

1   2

STAGE 3

RHYTHMIC EXERCISES

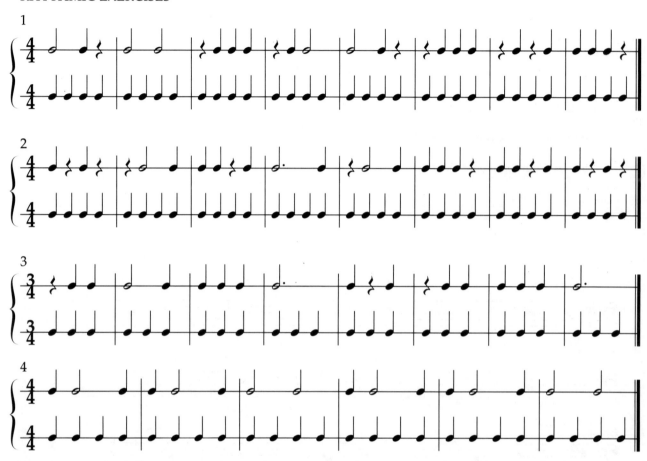

MELODIC EXERCISES

Mark:

PREPARED PIECE

1 How many beats is each dotted minim ($\natural$.) worth? ☐

2 How many beats is each minim ($\natural$) worth? ☐

3 How many beats does this rest ▬ occupy? ☐

4 What does *p* *(piano)* indicate? ☐

5 What does the sign ◁ *(crescendo)* indicate? ☐

6 What is the meaning of *Moderato?* ☐

Total: ☐

Mark: ☐

Prepared work total: ☐

Unprepared: ☐

Total: ☐

Running totals:

1	2	3

STAGE 4

RHYTHMIC EXERCISES

MELODIC EXERCISES

Mark: [ ]

PREPARED PIECE

1 What does $\frac{4}{4}$ indicate?

2 Clap the following rhythms:

3 What does *p* indicate?

4 What does *mf* indicate?

5 What does the sign ⟍ indicate?

6 What is the meaning of *Allegro moderato?*

Total:

Allegro moderato

Mark:

Prepared work total:

Unprepared:

Total:

Running totals:

1	2	3	4

STAGE 5

F major

Keep the key signature in mind, and check it at the beginning of each new line to remind yourself of the key.

Always notice scale and arpeggio patterns in the melody. Make sure you know your scales and arpeggios.

MELODIC EXERCISES

1

2

3

Mark:

PREPARED PIECE

1 In which key is the piece written? ☐

2 Which notes are affected by the key-signature? (Mark each with a cross) ☐

3 How many beats are there in each bar? ☐

4 What is the letter name of the first note in bar 4?

                         bar 5?

                         bar 7? ☐

5 What is the meaning of *Moderato con moto?* ☐

6 What do *dim. (diminuendo)* and *cresc. (crescendo)* indicate? ☐

Total: ☐

Mark: ☐

Prepared work total: ☐

Unprepared: ☐

Total: ☐

Running totals:

1	2	3	4	5

STAGE 6

RHYTHMIC EXERCISES

MELODIC EXERCISES

Mark:

PREPARED PIECE

1 How many beats are there in each bar?

2 In which key is the piece written?

3 Mark with a cross the notes affected by the key-signature.

4 What do the markings ꞈꞈ (bar 8) indicate?

5 Clap this rhythm:

6 Mark an accidental with an asterisk.

Total:

Andante grazioso

5

10

Mark:

Prepared work total:

Unprepared:

Total:

Running totals:

1	2	3	4	5	6

STAGE 7

RHYTHMIC EXERCISES

MELODIC EXERCISES

Mark:

PREPARED PIECE

1 In which key is the piece written?

2 Mark the F sharps with a cross.

3 What do the dots under and above the notes indicate?

4 What does *Allegretto* mean?

5 What does *cresc. (crescendo)* indicate?

6 Mark a tied note with an asterisk.

Total:

Allegretto

Mark:

Prepared work total:

Unprepared:

Total:

Running totals:

1	2	3	4	5	6	7

STAGE 8

For accurate sight-reading it is important to know when it will be best to count in sub-divisions of the beat. When more difficult rhythms occur, counting in sub-divisions will prove very helpful.

Count all the work in this stage in quavers.

RHYTHMIC EXERCISES

MELODIC EXERCISES

Mark:

PREPARED PIECE

1   In which key is the piece written? Play the appropriate scale.

2   What note values will you count and why?

3   Where does the music of the first two bars return? Mark the bars with a bracket.

4   How many beats will you count for the G in bar 2?

5   What is the letter name of the second note in bar 6?

6   Clap this rhythm:

Total:

Moderato

6

11

Mark:

Prepared work total:

Unprepared:

Total:

Running totals:

1	2	3	4	5	6	7	8

STAGE 9

B♭ major

RHYTHMIC EXERCISES

MELODIC EXERCISES

Mark: ☐

PREPARED PIECE

1 How many beats are there in each bar?

2 What does the marking ♩ indicate?

3 That does *mf* indicate?

4 What does the marking ♩ indicate?

5 What is the meaning of *Moderato, tempo di minuetto?*

6 Clap this rhythm:

Total:

Moderato, tempo di minuetto

mf

6

12

Mark:

Prepared work total:

Unprepared:

Total:

Running totals:

1	2	3	4	5	6	7	8	9

STAGE 10

RHYTHMIC EXERCISES

MELODIC EXERCISES

Mark:

PREPARED PIECE

1 In which note values will you count this piece?

2 What is the meaning of *Allegro ma non troppo?*

3 In which key is the piece written?

4 What does the sign 𝅗𝅥 indicate?

5 Mark an accidental with a cross.

6 What is the letter name of the last note in bar 12?

Total:

Allegro ma non troppo

dim.   mp

Mark:

Prepared work total:

Unprepared:

Total:

Running totals:

1	2	3	4	5	6	7	8	9	10

STAGE 11

RHYTHMIC EXERCISES

MELODIC EXERCISES

Mark:

PREPARED PIECE

1   In which key is the piece written?

2   How many beats are there in each bar?

3   Mark the note affected by the key-signature with a cross.

4   Mark with a bracket a bar in which the arpeggio of G major occurs.

5   What does *Allegro giocoso* mean?

6   Clap this rhythm:

Total:

Allegro giocoso

Mark:

Prepared work total:

Unprepared:

Total:

Running totals:

1	2	3	4	5	6	7	8	9	10	11

STAGE 12

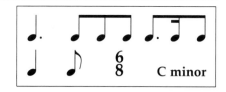

RHYTHMIC EXERCISES

MELODIC EXERCISES

Mark:

PREPARED PIECE

1 What is the meaning of the time signature?
   How many beats will you count in each bar?

2 In which key is the piece written?

3 Mark with a cross any notes affected by the key-signature.

4 For how many beats is the E (bars 7-8) held?

5 What is the meaning of *rall. (rallentando)?*

                          cresc. (crescendo)?

                          dim. (diminuendo)?

6 What does *Andante sostenuto* mean?

                                                    Total:

Andante sostenuto

                                                    Mark:

                              Prepared work total:

                                      Unprepared:

                                            Total:

Running totals:

1	2	3	4	5	6	7	8	9	10	11	12

CONCLUSION

A sight-reading checklist

Before you begin to play a piece at sight, always remember to consider the following:

1 Look at the key-signature.

2 Look at the time-signature.

3 Find the notes which need raising or lowering.

4 Take note of any accidentals.

5 Notice scale and arpeggio patterns.

6 Work out leger-line notes if necessary.

7 Notice dynamic and other markings.

8 Count one bar before you begin, to establish the speed.

When performing your sight-reading piece, always remember to:

1 Count yourself in with at least one bar in your chosen tempo and CONTINUE TO COUNT THROUGHOUT THE PIECE.

2 Keep going at a steady and even tempo.

3 Ignore mistakes.

4 Look ahead – at least to the next note.

5 Play *musically*.

UNPREPARED TESTS
PREPARATORY STAGE

1   Moderato

2   Andante

3   Moderato

STAGE 1

1   Andante

2   Moderato

3   Andante con moto

STAGE 2

1   Moderato

2   Allegretto

3   Tempo di Valse

STAGE 3

1   Moderato

2   Allegro

3   Allegretto

STAGE 4

1   Andante con moto

2   Alla marcia

3   Tempo di minuetto

STAGE 5

1   Marcato

2   Grazioso

3   Animato

STAGE 6

1   Andante

2   Allegretto

3   Moderato

STAGE 7

1   Alla marcia

2   Allegro giocoso

3   Allegro moderato

STAGE 8

1   Allegro moderato

2   Andante alla rumba

3   Moderato

STAGE 9

STAGE 10

1   Allegro marcato

2   Moderato

3   Lento con espressione

STAGE 11

1   Andante

2   Allegro giocoso

3   Moderato (scherzando)

STAGE 12

1   Allegretto con moto

2   Allegro moderato

3   Con moto